Choose to LIVE LIFE

Anita Pearce

anita pearce

choose

to live life

Choose to LIVE LIFE
Copyright © 2007, Anita Pearce

ISBN: 978-0-9783781-0-3

Cover design: designguys. *www.designguys.ca*
Book design: Andrew Mackay
Managing Editor: Beryl Henne

Printed in Canada

For more information, please contact:

Inspiration Ministries
Box 44
Margo, SK Canada S0A 2M0

www.inspirationministries.net

To you the reader,
as you enthusiastically pursue life,
choosing eternal values.

Table of Contents

Acknowledgements

I am abundantly blessed to have had the assistance of an excellent team of friends who have made this project possible. Their help and encouragement is treasured. These are people to whom I wish to express particular appreciation:

Leanne Simpson – for typing out the original sermon. Your faithful service is greatly appreciated.

Darlene Kienle – for being my loyal friend and colleague. Your affirmation and encouragement mean more to me than words can tell.

Alice Dutcyvich – for all the hours spent on the phone patiently correcting, advising, and encouraging. Your enthusiasm has sparked my inspiration and your thoroughness has challenged me to reach for excellence. Your friendship is a wonderful blessing.

Doreen Holdsworth – for your amazing expertise and willingness to assist in this project. Your help has been invaluable.

Several friends – for reading the manuscript and offering valuable counsel.

Introduction

To the casual observer she was an ordinary retired pastor's wife. She was badly bent with arthritis but insisted on hobbling twice a day to sit with her husband of over fifty years. He had just been placed in a nursing home after suffering a debilitating stroke. Her son had recently died of cancer. Major disappointments were arriving regularly.

Laying aside her own sorrows and conflicts, however, she always had time to listen to others. Acquaintances, some who had personalities that were quite difficult and demanding, constantly beat a path to her door for words of encouragement and understanding. Her home smelled of fresh baking and her smile warmly welcomed everyone.

Knowing a little of her personal heartbreak I once asked her, "How do you manage to be so consistently pleasant, even in such trying situations and with such attention-demanding people?"

"It's all a matter of choice," she replied.

God, in His wisdom and grace, has given the power of choice to every human being. The ability to decide our destiny includes taking responsibility for our attitudes, our behavior and our character. Our choices control the thoughts we think and develop the deepest values of our being. Recognizing this great gift of God can empower us to live life to the fullest with eternal impact.

This book is not meant to be an exhaustive resource, but rather an encouragement to recognize our highest potential. Some solutions presented may seem simplistic, but they are effective. There may be cases of mental illness or drug-induced behaviors that could suppress the power of choice. It is not my intention to address those situations.

The observations that I have included have changed and challenged me. It is my desire they will assist you, the reader, as you endeavor to walk the abundant life that is available in Christ.

Chapter One

Realizing the Power
of Choice

*Destiny is not a matter of chance;
it is a matter of choice.*

Whatever you are, be a good one.

Abraham Lincoln

She was somewhat radical. There was no doubt about it. My first impression was of a carefree teenager stretching the limits of fashion. Somewhat cautiously, I viewed her multiple piercings and streaked hair, but was quickly put at ease by her exuberant personality.

Her sister-in-law and I had dropped in to visit as we were driving through her city. She excitedly told of her involvement as youth pastor, of her work with troubled teens, and the amazing opportunities she could see everywhere to impact the youth of the city for Christ. Obviously her home had become the central station. A steady stream of teenagers came and went. As we spoke together, her quiet husband entertained their two busy children, one preschooler and one first grader.

Her eyes sparkled as she described her dreams-come-true. Her first music CD would be released soon. Special outreach weekends were being planned. There were involvements with worship seminars, youth retreats, and street ministry. I began to feel a little dizzy by her contagious enthusiasm for life.

However, when her sister-in-law asked about her health, there was a momentary pause. A rare series of physical attacks, including a brain tumor and kidney failure, had put her in the hospital frequently for several weeks at a time. With candor she admitted that the medical authorities could offer no solutions and very little hope. In spite of taking powerful medications twice a day, she was enduring chronic pain under the shadow of sudden death. As far as the doctors were concerned, it was impossible for her to be alive. They could offer no explanations or cures; only shake

16

their heads at the miracle she was living yet another day. It was obvious she was really living!

Financial setbacks, rejection by some peers, and personal disappointments have not deterred her. The responsibilities of family and ministry have only enflamed her passion for life and for loving Jesus. Constantly aware of its fragility, she has chosen to live life to its fullest for her allotted time.

In Deuteronomy 30:19 we read these words of Moses to the children of Israel:

> *I call heaven and earth to record this day against you, that I have set before you life and death, blessing and cursing: therefore choose life, that both thou and thy seed may live.*

The book of Deuteronomy is a series of sermons given by Moses before he died and before the people of Israel entered the Promised Land. This verse summarizes one of these messages. Here we find two powerful words: choose life.

Jesus gave a similar emphasis in Matthew 7:13, 14 when He taught,

Enter through the narrow gate. For wide is the gate and broad is the road that leads to destruction, and many enter through it. But small is the gate and narrow the road that leads to life (NIV).

Man is the crown of God's creation. Other creatures make choices based on instinct. In some cases their innate abilities can reason easier ways to procure sustenance. Some specialists would even identify a certain capacity for invention. However, the ability to make rational, moral choices with self-conscious and purposeful reflection is a gift unique to the human race.

Although we cannot always choose our circumstances, we have power to decide our reactions and attitudes in response to them.

The capacity to identify ourselves within each situation in life and determine our response is more potent than we may recognize. From our assimilated knowledge and experience, we are able to make calculations and

draw conclusions. Although we canno
choose our circumstances, we have p
decide our reactions and attitudes in res~ ~...~c to
them. It is that ability which enables us not just
to survive, but also to thrive in seemingly impossible situations. We are empowered to turn
lemons into lemonade.

Fred, a friend of mine, was the seventh of
eight children. When Fred was still very young,
his father was hospitalized and later died with
tuberculosis. His three elder brothers worked
hard to help provide for the impoverished family.
When he was five years old, his mother decided
to make a new life for herself—minus all of the
children. His twelve-year-old sister watched as
her mother drove off with her new boyfriend.
Without even a backward glance, she left the five
youngest children to fend for themselves. The
children were forced into foster homes until they
were sixteen—then they were obligated to live
and work on their own.

At the last foster home Fred learned about the
love of God. The options were clear. He could
become angry and bitter because of the unfairness

of his circumstances or he could choose to forgive and follow the ways of Christ. Thankfully, he made a wise decision. With God's help he found grace to forgive his mother and others who had taken advantage of his childhood helplessness. Later in life, he married and was blessed with a loving family. Although he had suffered during his last years with the debilitating ravages of ALS, also known as Lou Gehrig's disease, he chose cheerfulness and died with dignity, ever optimistic. The ashes of painful experience were turned into beauty of character because of proper choices.

Although circumstances may be excruciating, it is always within our power to decide what we will become because of them. We have the potential to determine our reactions. Dignity of character is ours to create and control. We can soar like eagles even if we feel we work with turkeys!

On one occasion I was deeply disappointed by an unexpected change of plans. Sitting alone in a restaurant, I was suddenly deluged by a great wave of sympathy for myself. I began to think of all that had gone wrong in this situation and how acute my discouragement was. Very rapidly my mind conjured up an ever-increasing number of injustices and sorrows until I struggled to keep the tears from diluting my coffee. Outside the window fallen leaves were blowing around on that dreary day—add a little sentimental country music, a half-cooked hamburger, and a dead cell-phone battery. The good cheer of the breezy little waitress got on my nerves. I was far from home and who would care where I was anyway. My pity party was turning into a rave.

Passing the mirror in the washroom I caught sight of my face—quite a droopy specimen. I gloomily meditated a moment on the reflection, "If I look this bad now, what am I going to be like in twenty years? My worst look now will someday be the best!" Life was passing me by.

Like a bolt of lightning, a thought flashed through my head. I could choose to let life drearily drag on, permitting the wrinkles on my face to reflect my shriveled soul—or I could turn the challenges of today into the victories of tomorrow. It was obvious that I could feel sorry for myself or I could enjoy life to the maximum, but I couldn't do both at the same time.

This ego pampering was ridiculous. Miraculously, I shed ten years as I laughed at myself in the mirror. Maybe it was the lost weight of the self-pity, but I felt at least twenty pounds lighter as I got back into my car. Choosing a positive mind-set in the difficult circumstance produced renewed energy to pursue solutions.

We are responsible for our choices

It is of primary importance that we recognize that we *are* the result of our personal choices. We cannot blame the circumstances, or the government, or family, or race—nothing and no one—for who we *are*. No matter where we are or what we experience, our reaction in any situation is always our decision.

Although some circumstances of life may enhance character or happiness, *ultimately the person I become will be the person I decide to be.* I am today the result of my choices yesterday; I will be tomorrow the result of my choices today. I must take full responsibility for my decisions.

The story is told of a small boy who was standing on a cat's tail. The cat was complaining loudly. When his mother told the little fellow to stop pulling the cat's tail he replied, "I'm not pulling the cat's tail. I'm just standing on it. He's doing all the pulling!" We naturally prefer to pass the buck and declare ourselves innocent.

Either by introspection or comparison with others, we may find who we *are* to be less than what we desire. We search to find an escape from our personal responsibility. We may blame our predicaments on other people or institutions for producing *who* we have become. In doing so, we only succeed in condemning ourselves to continued disappointment. It is the decisions that we have made that have formed the character we now possess. Release, forgiveness, and freedom can only be ours when we choose to own the problems and receive the solutions.

It is the decisions that we have made that have formed the character we now possess.

A secular newspaper[1] contained an excerpt from an interview with Aleksandr Solzhenitsyn, author of *The Gulag Archipelago*. Mr. Solzhenitsyn had served time and endured torture in Soviet prison camps because of his political convictions. His statement could be summarized thus: "No government, prison, or prejudice can take away our power of choice. Our reactions and attitudes to any circumstance are always our choice."

Some may say, "But you don't understand the difficulty of my situation." In even the most severe crises we have the choice to respond positively or negatively. Who we truly are is revealed by the decisions we make that produce the resulting reactions.

Two elderly women who live near each other are experiencing the complications of advancing age. Both have endured disasters, diseases, and disappointments. However, their reactions to the setbacks of life have been as different as day is from night. While one complains incessantly of her pains and grievances, the other brings comfort and laughter to everyone she meets. One woman has become increasingly isolated. Friends who enjoy her good cheer surround the other.

24

Steven Covey wrote, "Our behavior is a function of our decisions, not our conditions. We can subordinate feeling to value. We have the initiative and the responsibility to make things happen."[2] Later he added, "It is not what happens to us, but our response to what happens to us that hurts us."[3]

Knowledge empowers our choices

Knowledge has a powerful influence in directing our choices. We gain knowledge both consciously and subconsciously, from various observations, intellectual study, and past experience. People use this collected information to calculate conclusions. Proper knowledge gives us power to make appropriate decisions. For instance, knowing that the road is icy, and that the improper use of brakes will put the car into a skid prepares us to drive more cautiously under those conditions. Therefore, we make choices to adjust our driving habits based on the knowledge we possess.

We know that speaking insulting words or reacting in an angry manner in hurtful situations has the potential to explode out of control. With this knowledge we choose to keep our temper in check and our lips zipped—if we are smart!

To find knowledge that will help us in practical decisions such as how to build a house or fix a car, we must go to the sources who know at least as much as we and hopefully a little more. However, when we are searching for knowledge of God, for methods of building character and ways of mending broken hearts, the Word of God offers us information we need. The Bible declares in Proverbs 9:10, [the] *"Fear of the* LORD *is the foundation of wisdom. Knowledge of the Holy One results in good judgment"* (TLB).

As we nurture our relationship with God through the principles and promises of His Word, we begin to understand His plan, His will, and His ways. Committing the Word of God to memory can make invaluable nuggets of help and hope readily available in time of need. Spending time in God's presence and studying His Word develops closeness to Him and sensitivity in making wise decisions.

Paul and Silas gave us an excellent example of choosing positive reactions in the face of strenuous difficulties. Their knowledge of God's love and mercy gave them hope—and a song in the night. They had been preaching in the city of Philippi where a young slave possessed by a spirit of divination was set free as a result of their ministry. Her owners were furious. They had the two men arrested, whipped, and put into the dungeon. The preachers' discomfort in the darkness of a filthy first-century prison, with bleeding backs and probably without food or sanitation, would be difficult to imagine. Yet Acts 16:25 records: "...*at midnight Paul and Silas prayed, and sang praises unto God....*"

Paul had a totally different perspective about stocks and bonds! (His investments were truly out of this world—working for God does not often produce a high salary, but He has a great retirement plan!) Silas and he determined to pray and put their trust in God. Their song sprang from their knowledge of God and their choice to rejoice in the Lord in spite of their distress.

27

Through the Word of God we are supplied with knowledge that can direct us in making positive decisions.

Discovering the tremendous potential activated by positive choices can be a life-changing experience. The identity and character that we make of ourselves, our *being,* is our responsibility to create. Through the Word of God we are supplied with knowledge that can direct us in making positive decisions. With Christ, we can learn how to live on the higher road of life.

Questions for Practical Application

1. Can you name individuals who have impacted you by their positive choices in face of difficult circumstances?

2. What have been the primary sources of knowledge from which you have calculated your decisions? Have these resources led you to make constructive or destructive conclusions?

3. Can you identify areas in which you need to take responsibility for your decisions?

4. How have you become a better person by the choices you have made? Can you describe how and when some of those character-defining moments happened?

5. What are some ways you plan to incorporate the power of choice into your daily experiences?

Challenge

I call heaven and earth to record this day against you, that I have set before you life and death, blessing and cursing: therefore choose life, that both thou and thy seed may live.

Deuteronomy 30:19

Chapter Two

Releasing the Hand of God

If we do no more than we've always done,
we'll have no more than we've always had.

In major experiences throughout life, and particularly in relation to our spiritual condition, our decisions release the hand of God to work in our circumstances. Sometimes we seek to justify our passivity by using the excuse that we are waiting for God to move. Truly He is sovereign. His power is unlimited. Yet the Word of God is filled with evidence that He waits for us to use the power of choice and act in faith. When we do so, He moves heaven and earth to work on our behalf. This is manifested in the following four areas.

The Conversion of the Soul

The message of the Gospel is the good news that although we are separated from God by our sin, through the death of Jesus on the cross we can find forgiveness. We can experience the overcoming power of the resurrected Christ in a living and personal relationship with God. We can have peace with God.

Romans 3:23 states, "...*all have sinned, and come short of the glory of God.*" Separating us from God is the great gulf of sin. The Bible tells us pointedly that sin includes all of human pride, rebellion, selfishness—all that cause us to come short of God's perfection in whose image we were initially created. By our own works we can never be free from this burden of evil. However, by the sacrifice of the sinless Son of God upon the cross, sin's penalty was paid in full. Jesus took our place of punishment in order to purchase our pardon.

When we hear the Gospel we begin to understand the inescapable necessity of repentance. All that is received from God comes directly through repentance and faith in Christ. Whether we acknowledge God or not, does not change our personal responsibility before Him. When we have acted in rebellion to God's Word, when we have sinned, there can be no release from our guilt without owning up to it. We must repent with contrition and humility. True repentance produces a change of heart, of attitude, and of char-

True repentance produces a change of heart, of attitude, and of character as the power of Christ works in us.

acter as the power of Christ works in us. The Bible says in 1 John 1:9, *"If we confess our sins, he is faithful and just to forgive us our sins, and to cleanse us from all unrighteousness."*

The good news is that Jesus can save even you, but you must respond to Him. The Holy Spirit may call and convict you for days, weeks, or years. You are conscious of Him drawing you to Christ. However, you cannot be converted until you make the choice and surrender your

33

will to the Lord Jesus. At that moment, the Holy Spirit is released to work in you. You are cleansed. You are set free. You are changed. Romans 10:13 promises, *"For whosoever shall call upon the name of the Lord shall be saved."*

Multiplied millions of people have experienced the soul-saving, life-changing presence of Jesus at their moment of submission to His Lordship. I well remember one young lady who came forward for prayer at the end of a service I was conducting. When I asked what her request was, she burst into tears and sobbed, "I'm tired of running from God. I'm tired of running from my mother's prayers! I want to give my life to Christ." As she prayed, the transforming love of God reached into her heart. A miracle happened and she was converted. At her surrender, the power of salvation was released.

The Conflicts of Sanctification

After conversion, there are problems and struggles that will be encountered. We need the empowerment of God's grace to work with us as we set out to overcome them. Although all of heaven's resources are available by faith, some people are never freed from their bondages because they never make the solid decision to destroy them.

David went to visit his brothers in the army of Israel. They were fighting against the Philistines. Day after day the giant, Goliath, taunted them. David recognized that this giant was not just defying Israel, but Almighty God. David made the choice to face-off with the giant. When he made that decision, the hand of God was released to enable him to vanquish Goliath.

Once when I was speaking in a street mission, two drunken men responded for prayer. Together the pastor and I prayed with each of them. They both cried with sorrow for their state. Later we learned that one of them went through treatment, became sober, and was delivered to live a wholesome life. The other never progressed. I came to the conclusion that one of these men wanted to be free and the other did not.

Another gentleman, who had given his life to Christ, struggled nearly eighteen years with his tobacco habit. He often came for prayer asking for deliverance. One night after prayer at the church, while sitting on the edge of his bed smoking his middle-of-the-night cigarette, he whimpered to the Lord, "Why don't You set me free?"

The Lord's answer was suddenly loud and clear in his heart, "Because you don't want to be free!" He fell to his knees in true repentance and was delivered on the spot!

Of course one may use the excuse, "I can't help doing what I do." I challenge you to remember some of those incidents. Honestly reconstruct your reactions in difficult situations, for example, the moment of explosive anger. Frame-by-frame roll back the video of the experience. Put the arm back down by your side, unclench the fist, close the mouth, stuff the words back down the throat. Roll the picture back until the first flash of heat in the belly. Do you remember? You made a choice. Instead of turning away, counting to ten, or softly replying, you let the heat rise, the words be spoken, the clenched fist wave in the air.

Although temptation may be great and internal pressures seem irresistible, ultimately the actions that we take are those that we permit.

36

There is a sequence that creates the outcome. Our decision determines the result.

It is true that there may be need for assistance to help us overcome some deeply rooted habits. It may be necessary to find a trusted confidant or circle of friends to whom we can bare our hearts and become account-able. However, to seek help always demands a choice.

Those working in counseling or psychiatric services have long concluded that it is impossible to aid people who really do not want to be helped. Unless there is a profound desire for change and determination to achieve a goal, there will be no transformation.

Unless there is a profound desire for change and determination to achieve a goal, there will be no transformation.

Teen Challenge has established many highly successful drug and alcohol rehabilitation pro-grams. People can be referred to this organization or be given information about it. However, individuals are not considered until they personally request help by contacting a center, make the effort to fill out the application forms, and take full responsibility for their actions. By putting the onus on those seeking help, Teen Challenge insists that they take the initial steps toward radical change.

When we make the uncompromising decision to face up to enslaving evil habits, unwholesome imaginations, undisciplined temperaments—and destroy these giants in our lives—the hand of God is released to set us free. Those who are transformed are those who take a definitive stand to defeat the destructive patterns in their lives. Others excuse their behavior and stay in bondage.

The Change of Situation

Human beings are creatures of habit. We are often uncomfortable with any changes that take place in our environment. Change is frightening. It disturbs our comfort zones. However, everything in life changes except the fact of change itself. We must embrace change in order to expand, adapt, and experience growth.

The Serenity Prayer reads, "God grant me the grace to accept the things I cannot change, the courage to change the things I can, and the wisdom to know the difference." These are wise words well spoken. There are circumstances that cannot be changed—*we* must change our way of thinking, our attitudes, and our reactions.

A woman had been extremely frustrated with her marriage. For a number of years she had nagged her husband to change his ways. Nothing happened. She slid into sullen sulks. Their relationship was being eroded by anger and unreasonable expectations on both sides. One day the revelation came to her that she could not change him. She had, however, the power to make changes within herself. With a prayer of repentance, she set out to live and forgive with a loving and accepting attitude toward her husband. It took a lot of work and perseverance. To her amazement she realized that when her attitude changed, some of his irritating ways became endearing traits. He had not changed; she had!

In other scenarios we can and must make a difference in the circumstance. It has been stated that we deserve what we tolerate. Often we resist change until the pain level of our situation becomes so intense that we cannot stand it any longer. In those moments, we desperately pray for God to change something or move somebody. The solution is frozen, however, until we make a choice to act. When we make decisions, God's power is released to bring solutions.

Often we resist change until the pain level of our situation becomes so intense that we cannot stand it any longer.

For several years I lived in a twelve-by-fifty-foot mobile home. It was a cozy but somewhat crowded nest. A twelve-by-sixteen-foot addition to one side served as an office. As the ministry expanded, the spaces were filled with office equipment and stock. The six-hundred-square-foot living space was shrinking rapidly. Hints were made that things were getting too squished for two secretaries and me to work in the office. Then I was informed that the new photocopier would not fit into the office. There was no option. It would have to sit in the middle of my living room. That was the limit. I was not going to live the rest of my life with a photocopier in my living room! My comfort zone was no longer comfortable!

A debate with many questions filled my mind. "Is the relief that I will find from the change in situation worth the price I will have to pay?" Then the practical voice, "Where will I get the money to buy another house?" As I stepped out by faith to make the purchase, I felt the peace of God. Within days everything fell into place. An excellent home and facility were mine. The photocopier fit nicely in the office—out of my living room! I had been forced to make a move, and in doing so, found something far better than I had dreamed. The solution was realized when a decision for change was made.

The high school was located next door to the church in a small town where a friend of mine was the pastor. A large group of teenagers would sit on the church steps during school breaks, leaving graffiti and cigarette butts around the entrance. Although he was highly irritated, one day the pastor hit on a solution. He made a room available in the church where, under supervision, the youth could play board games and be free to hang out. The results were phenomenal. Within a short time he had befriended many of them. The power of the Gospel, manifested through his love and understanding, transformed their lives. That wise pastor realized that by choosing proactive involvement he could defuse the situation and bring constructive progress.

The shrill screech of a rusty hinge irritated me every time I opened the door. Always in a rush, I neglected to do anything about it for several weeks. Finally it squeaked once too often and I attacked it with an oil can. Instant relief made me wonder why I had put up with it for so long. Whenever we put things off until tomorrow, I suppose it would be good advice to ask ourselves what we did about it yesterday! If it is in our power to transform the situation, we need to make some choices that will produce positive results.

The Call to Service

As we follow Christ, fulfilling His will becomes increasingly important to us. Our greatest desire is to please Him; we long to do His bidding. The question often comes, "How can we know the will of God for our lives?"

Jesus established priorities in Matthew 6:33, *"...seek ye first the kingdom of God, and his righteousness; and all these things shall be added unto you."* When we make God and His purposes our primary focus in life, He has promised that He will provide everything else that we may need. His supply is more than sufficient for our physical, emotional, and material requirements. Necessities fall into proper perspective as we make Christ the center of our lives: where He guides, He provides.

There are many resources that can assist us in discovering specific direction in His service. There is agreement that some of the initial steps include: studying God's Word, never compromising the peace of God, and receiving counsel from trusted spiritual leadership. However, it is my experience that the realization of His will only comes as we make choices and act by faith.

I often worried that I might miss God's direction for my life. What if I made the wrong decision? Then this definition was presented to me, "The will of God is to take the next possible human step with your heart open to God." That may sound simplistic, but it is a good starting point. I have been told that it is harder for the earnest-seeking child of God to miss God's will than to find it.

When I was a teenager, I had a sorrel cowpony named Dixie. Like many people, that horse could exhibit a stubborn streak. If she didn't want to go, she would plant her feet firmly under the barn door where I could not get onto her back. I could tug on the reins, pull her, call her...but she wouldn't budge. Then I made the discovery that if I just pulled hard enough on the reins to swing her head around facing her tail, she would have to take a step or she would lose her balance. Once she made that first step, we would make a circle out the door, where I would hop on, and off we'd go. It was impossible to guide that animal when she wasn't moving.

As a child I would sit in my father's car, pretending to drive by turning the steering wheel this way and that. In imagination I had covered hundreds of kilometers, but in reality I hadn't moved a single centimeter.

You may have grandiose ideas of what to do with your life, but you need to make progress by taking action. For example, if your sink is full of dirty dishes and your house is a mess, don't sit in despair crying to know the will of God. Wash the dishes! Doing what is in front of you—taking the next possible human step—is fulfilling the will of God.

Sometimes we are guilty of making our walk with God so mystical that we are not realistic. Proverbs 16:9 states, *"A man's heart deviseth his way: but the LORD directeth his steps."* The Living Bible renders it this way, *"We should make plans—counting on God to direct us."* You may be pleading, "Oh God, please show me what steps You want me to take."

He is saying, "I would love to, if you would

just make a few!" He waits for your choices in order to release His guidance.

He waits for your choices in order to release His guidance.

When Abraham's servant was sent to find a wife for Isaac, he prayed earnestly for God to direct him. Arriving in Abraham's homeland, he was guided to the very family for whom he searched. He was assured that Rebekah was the one chosen by God for Isaac. In Genesis 24:27 we read that the servant said, "*...I being in the way, the LORD led me to the house of my master's brethren.*"

You can't steer a car if it is not moving. You can't ride a bicycle standing still. Make some decisions; take some action. It is as you make plans and choices that God can direct your steps. He will provide the opportunities of where He wants you to go and what He wants you to do. That is the promise found in Proverbs 3:5, 6: "*Trust in the LORD with all thine heart; and lean not unto thine own understanding. In all thy ways acknowledge him, and he shall direct thy paths."* He is big enough to open right doors and close wrong ones.

In each of these areas—salvation, sanctification, situation, and service—our choices are the catalysts that effectively release divine intervention. As we respond with surrender to the gentle voice of God within, His power is released to fulfill His highest purposes in our lives.

Questions for Practical Application

1. Have you observed lack of progress in the lives of some of your acquaintances because of indecision?

2. Have you surrendered to the claims of Christ upon your life? If not, why not now?

3. Are there giants, such as destructive habits, in your life that remain unchallenged? What do you plan to do about them?

4. Can you identify present situations that are stagnant because they are waiting for your decisions? When do you plan to proceed?

5. Have you made specific steps to accomplish what you sense is God's will for your life?

Challenge

...seek ye first the kingdom of God, and his righteousness; and all these things shall be added unto you.

Matthew 6:33

Chapter Three

Choosing Life or Death

If you seek your Lord Jesus in all things, you will truly find Him: but if you seek yourself, you will find yourself; and that will be to your own great loss.

Thomas A. Kempis

Parents endeavor to teach their children the ethics and manners that will help them to one day be responsible adults. There is something of the rebel in human nature, however, that begins to manifest even in toddlers. As they explore their world and are told they must not touch this, they must not go there, or must not do that, inherently it seems those are the very directions pursued! As they grow, this desire to push the limits, to taste and try the forbidden, often brings grief to their parents as well as to themselves.

My three-year-old nephew was caught red-handed, standing on a chair with his hand buried up to the elbow in the cookie jar. As his mother advanced he grabbed as many as he could. "Didn't do it Mommy," he repeated as he hopped off the chair and ran, stuffing cookies into his mouth as fast as he could!

We can see this rebellious tendency from creation. In the Garden of Eden, Adam and Eve were told not to partake of the fruit of the tree of knowledge of good and evil. At the urging of the serpent, that tree became of paramount interest. The serpent promised that if they would eat of this fruit they would receive the abilities of God to differentiate between good and evil.

For God doth know that in the day ye eat thereof, then your eyes shall be opened, and ye shall be as gods, knowing good and evil. And when the woman saw that the tree was good for food, and that it was pleasant to the eyes, and a tree to be desired to make

one wise, she took of the fruit thereof,
and did eat, and gave also unto her hus-
band with her; and he did eat (Genesis
3:5, 6).

Whatever was the type of fruit is quite unim-
portant. It was their act of disobedience in partak-
ing of the forbidden fruit that immediately
"opened their eyes" to the iniquity from which
their loving Creator desired to shield them. The
sense of guilt in response to their rebellion suddenly made our first parents cognizant of evil.
Their once-pure conscience agonized at the aware-
ness of sin; they hid to escape from God's presence.

And they heard the voice of the LORD
God *walking in the garden in the cool of*
the day: and Adam and his wife hid
themselves from the presence of the
LORD God *amongst the trees of the gar-*
den (Genesis 3:8).

In the context of right versus wrong, human
nature always gravitates to explore the wrong.

In the context of right versus wrong, human nature always gravitates to explore the wrong.

Society attempts to maintain order by the rule of law. The law condemns wrongdoing and seeks to imprint minds with structures of acceptable behavior. However, there is a basic flaw. The human heart is drawn to the forbidden like vultures to a carcass. The search for the right is always an uphill struggle involving rules and regulations. As Paul discovered, the laws that were meant for good bring bondage and death due to our inability to live within their boundaries without God's intervention (Romans 7).

There is another paradigm—the paradigm of life versus death. When we understand that the end result of proper choices produce life rather than death, the motivation to follow the way of life is powerfully fortified. When we acknowledge that every inappropriate decision has the potential of death, it serves to reinforce the desire for life. This, of course, results in transformed

54

attitudes. The knowledge of good and evil brings destruction; the choice of life over death sets us free to live life. God has not laid out the rules of His kingdom to keep us from enjoying the good times. It is not His plan to keep us from having fun. Rather, His principles are to protect us from the brokenness and the bondages that are hall-marks of the way of death.

How can I choose the way of life?

The voice of God always speaks through the conscience. Human reasoning often disputes with the conscience, trying desperately to justify ungodly actions. We attempt to quiet the voice within. The guilt that results from rebellion to our conscience brings loneliness, then despair. This is the way of death.

We need to carefully evaluate the end result of our choices, attitudes, and actions. The way of life will always bring beauty of character and uncom-promised integrity. The peace of God is found only on this path of life. Jesus said in John 14:27, *"Peace I leave with you, my peace I give unto you: not as the world giveth, give I unto you...."*

When confronted with decisions we need to ask ourselves, "What will the end be?"

When confronted with decisions we need to ask ourselves, "What will the end be? Will the harvest we reap be one of blessing or cursing? Will it leave us filled with remorse and regrets, or with comfort and contentment? Will I be a better person for the decision I make?"

We must also contemplate the eternal dimension. When dealing with the reality of death— and our destiny beyond the grave—we should carefully ponder the eternal impact of our choices. In that day of reckoning, with our lives in review, would we be haunted by shame? Thank God, that through repentance and faith in Christ, there is a provided remedy for our guilt, but this does not absolve us from the personal responsibility of making choices that would be pleasing to Him.

A popular question among Christian youth has been, "What would Jesus do?" We inherently know that whatever would be acceptable to Him will always produce virtue and a pure conscience within us. This is the way of life.

I watched as a handsome young man was warned repeatedly about the friends he was hanging out with. Several concerned acquaintances tried in vain to persuade him not to continue in the direction he was going. Somewhat arrogantly he refused advice and determined to go his own way. That was many years ago. Today his addictions have destroyed his health and he is serving time for murder. Someone has aptly stated, "Sin will take you farther than you want to go, keep you longer than you want to stay, and cost you more than you want to pay." The writer of Proverbs declares in chapter 16, verse 25, *"There is a way that seems right to a man, but in the end it leads to death"* (NIV).

As a teenager, my peers were stretching their wings of independence. When the temptations to test the forbidden were placed before me, the example and teaching of godly friends and family helped me to see the futility, the emptiness, which would be the end result of these activities.

In one particular instance while driving home from church with my brother, we came upon an accident caused by a group of young people who had been driving while drunk. The most powerful influence was not what was right or wrong about the situation; rather, I could clearly see that the result of their lifestyle was the way of vanity and death. By considering my choices, with the end in view, I was empowered to resist many temptations. I earnestly desired the path that would produce quality and character. I have no regrets for the decisions that have brought profound fulfillment to me.

When we refer to the *way of life*, it always corresponds to what is right and virtuous; the *way of death* to that which is wrong and vain. By recognizing the principle of *choices that produce life* we rise to a higher standard, to a sweeter melody, to a lighter heart. Deep satisfaction, peace, and freedom are the end result. The race is well worth the reward.

Questions for Practical Application

1. Can you name individuals whose inappropriate choices have brought unnecessary pain?

2. Have you acknowledged your mistakes? What actions are you making to reconcile blunders and follow the way of life rather than the way of death?

3. Can you recall moments when you chose long-term values and virtues rather than momentary but destructive impulses?

4. What are some guidelines that have helped you make life-producing choices?

5. How often do you evaluate your life in the light of eternity?

6. What advice would you give to those contemplating life-impacting decisions?

7. Can you name individuals who impressed you because they made decisions based on principle rather than expediency?

Challenge

Enter through the narrow gate. For wide is the gate and broad is the road that leads to destruction, and many enter through it. But small is the gate and narrow the road that leads to life.

Matthew 7:13, 14; NIV

Chapter Four

Having a *Be* Attitude

The greatest discovery of any generation is that a human being can alter his life by altering his attitude.

William James

I wept that I had no shoes until I met a man who had no feet.

Ancient Persian saying

Viktor Frankl survived great physical and emotional suffering during the Nazi holocaust. While being humiliated and tortured, he made this discovery:

We who lived in concentration camps can remember the men who walked through the huts comforting others, giving away their last piece of bread. They may have been few in number, but they offer sufficient proof that everything can be taken from a man but one thing: the last of the human freedoms—to choose one's attitude in any given set of circumstances, to choose one's own way.[4]

Our attitudes toward life, work, and family are always ours to determine. The disposition of our mind powerfully influences our reactions in the various situations of life. After initial impulses and first impressions begin to wane, our sustained responses will be shaped by our chosen attitudes.

It can be somewhat self-deceiving to use the phrase, "I have to do…" or "I have to be…." The truer words are, "I have chosen to do…" or "I have chosen to be…." What we actually do day-by-day reveals our priorities and choices. An excuse has been defined as "a lack of desire." Often we make excuses to escape from unappealing suggestions. In reality, we are using the excuse to indirectly express our preferences. Profound desire will find solutions. We can always find the time and means to do what we really want to do.

Some face their workday with a sense of drudgery lamenting, "I can't stand my work, but

I have to do it." Take a break and look around. There are probably dozens of people who would count it a privilege to work at your job and receive your paycheck! You have the health, the strength, and the ability to do what many cannot. You don't *have* to do the job; you *get* to do it! It has been well stated that the secret of happiness is not to do what you like to do, but to learn to like what you have to do.

A wife may say, "I have to pick up this man's clothes." No, you don't. There are probably fifty women who would love to pick up that man's clothes! You have the opportunity to do what others only dream of!

Employers prefer workers who exhibit excellence of disposition. Some people may have all the know-how, but because of a bad attitude they never advance. We are admonished in Colossians 3:23, "*...whatsoever ye do, do it heartily, as to the Lord, and not unto men.*"

A middle-aged man who had rarely worked at the same job for more than a few months, had recently quit yet another enterprise. When asked why, he quickly listed all of his grievances and blamed bosses and colleagues for his dissatisfaction. It was apparent to everyone except himself that the true problem was his own arrogant and insubordinate attitude.

Pastor and author Chuck Swindoll shares keen wisdom when he writes:

> I believe the single most significant decision I can make on a day-to-day basis is my choice of attitude. It is more important than my past, my education, my bankroll, my successes or failures, fame or pain, what other people think of me or say about me; my circumstances, or my position. Attitude is that "single string" that keeps me going or cripples my progress. It alone fuels my fire or assaults my hope. When my attitudes are right, there's no barrier too high, valley too deep, no dream too extreme, no challenge too great for me.[5]

Apostle Paul expresses his choice of attitude in Philippians 4:11-13:

...For I have learned to be content whatever the circumstances. I know what it is to be in need, and I know what it is to have plenty. I have learned the secret of being content in any and every situation, whether well fed or hungry, whether living in plenty or in want. I can do everything through him who gives me strength (NIV).

Out of ourselves

The "Me Generation" is the term coined to describe the intense selfishness of modern society. The consumerism mentality seeks instant gratification for every sensual desire. Our relationships, accomplishments, or purchases earn merit depending on how well they feed our ego. This attitude pervades our choice of goals and unfortunately decides many of our values. If either circumstances or people do not satisfactorily meet our expectations, we lash out in disgust and anger or shrivel with bitterness and disillusionment.

Selfishness and all of its relatives—self-pity, self-centeredness, self-righteousness, and self-sensitivity, which flatter the ego in a vain effort to produce happiness—only create an unattainable mirage. When we permit our attitudes to be determined by the "what-we-get-out-of-it" mentality, we become slaves to ourselves, unable to find the light and love we seek. No slave driver is as cruel as our own selfishness.

When we choose to reach out of ourselves—deny ourselves—we find liberty and fulfillment.

By contrast, when we choose to reach out of ourselves—deny ourselves—we find liberty and fulfillment. Jesus taught this principle in Luke 9:24, *"For whosoever will save his life shall lose it: but whosoever will lose his life for my sake, the same shall save it."*

I have had ample opportunity to try to practice what I preach. I confess I don't always succeed in having the proper attitude. Some situations present a great deal of inconvenience, discomfort,

and loneliness. It would be easy to
pity, to complain, or to blame oth
pointment. In fact, I have discovere
deal of loneliness really is self-pity in disguise.

Barbara Johnson is a gifted writer whose
amusing books bring good cheer and encouragement to many. One could scarcely imagine the
pain of her personal experience. One son was
killed in Vietnam, one by a drunken driver.
Another son's rejection brought great anguish.
Rather than succumbing to depression and
despair, out of her brokenness she established a
ministry to hurting parents—bringing joy and
hope to others.

The following e-mail was forwarded to me. It
reminded me that the best thing to have in a bad
situation is a good attitude.

- People are unreasonable, illogical, and self-
  centered. Love them anyway.
- If you do good, people will accuse you of
  selfish, ulterior motives. Do good anyway.
- If you are successful, you will win false
  friends and true enemies. Succeed anyway.

67

- The good you do today may be forgotten tomorrow. Do good anyway.
- Honesty and frankness make you vulnerable. Be honest anyway.
- The person with the biggest ideas can be shot down by the person with the smallest mind. Think big anyway.
- What you spend years building may be destroyed overnight. Build anyway.
- People really need help but may attack you if you help them. Help people anyway.
- Give the world the best you have and in some ways you may fail. Give the world the best you have anyway.[6]

While staying in a home in France, I saw this note tacked to the wall. There was no source or author listed, but the message has profoundly impacted my life. The article was entitled, *Here is my Testimony*.

I have given myself entirely to Jesus Christ my Saviour. I asked for health that ght do great things. He gave me infirmity that I might do better things. I asked for wealth that I might be happy. He gave me poverty that I might be really free. I asked for a companion that I might not live alone. He gave me a heart to love everyone. I asked for everything that might fill my life with joy. He gave me life so that I could enjoy all things. I have had nothing of all that I asked, but I have had all for which I profoundly hoped.

Choices determine our thoughts

Our thoughts are controlled by our choices. We can choose to discipline our thought patterns: to change our perspective, to control our emotions, to create our character.

Choosing what we think can change our perspective. Some situations arise that can put us in a disagreeable frame of mind.

We can choose to discipline our thought patterns.

We become agitated and irritable. However, we can transform our entire outlook by making the choice to turn our thoughts in a positive direction. A friend rather dryly observed, "Even if you've been fishing for three hours and haven't caught anything except poison ivy and sunburn, you're still better off than the worm."

I continue to learn that I have the power to determine in my mind and heart that I can, if I will, make the best of unpleasant or undesirable circumstances. I must hold my tongue, lift up my heart, and choose to be cheerful. On one occasion in a foreign country I left a beauty salon in a huff. The hairdresser had not cut my hair the way I wanted and I was irritated. Not speaking the language very well, I could not even tell her how annoyed I was! For a couple of hours I fumed and fussed about this change of hairdo. Later that evening I met with a group of people. A handsome (and eligible) gentleman casually mentioned that he really liked my hairstyle. I had an instant paradigm shift. I decided then and there it was probably the nicest job any hairdresser had ever done!

Our emotions follow our thoughts. That explains why we can shed tears of sadness, laugh at amusing incidents, become angry at perceived injustice, and then feel alarmed or uncertain—all in a matter of minutes! We must not make decisions or establish attitudes based on our feelings. Emotions are often undependable and fickle.

Apostle Paul gave an excellent outline of the thoughts that produce wholesome living. In Philippians 4:8 he states,

> *Finally, brothers, whatever is true, whatever is noble, whatever is right, whatever is pure, whatever is lovely, whatever is admirable—if anything is excellent or praiseworthy—think about such things* (NIV).

In her book, *Loving God with All Your Mind*, Elizabeth George describes how this verse brought transformation within her. She recognized the command, "*...whatever is true...think about such things.*" When she began to apply the Biblical principle of permitting only thoughts of what is *true* and *real* to filter her perceptions of the past, the present, the future, the failures, and the successes, even about God, herself, and others, she was radically changed. She states,

> You can choose to think thoughts about God and life's situations that are not true…or you can choose to love God with all your mind and think the truths stated in Scripture. The next time you feel yourself slipping from confidence to cowardice, from control to emotion, from the strength of spiritual mental health to frailty of spirit, review the resources you have as a child of God. In times of trauma and testing, choose to fill your mind with what is true. Choose to love God.[7]

If we let it, our imagination can run wild, picturing all manner of hideous happenings—most prefixed with the words, "What if" or "If only." There have been moments when I have been transfixed with anxieties that were totally fabricated by my imagination. The images dancing in my head were neither true nor real. It was like being attacked by my shadow—and my emotions were left shredded and in tatters. However, when I chose to put those destructive ideas out of my mind, and concentrated on what I was actually experiencing, I found emotional stamina and courage.

Our character is created from the habitual thoughts we permit.

Our character is created from the habitual thoughts we permit. We can't help it when the birds fly over our heads, but when they start to build a nest in our hair we can do something about it. Many thoughts flitter through our brains; it is our decision which ones we capture. Jesus said in Mark 7:21-23,

> *For from within, out of men's hearts, come evil thoughts, sexual immorality, theft, murder, adultery, greed, malice, deceit, lewdness, envy, slander, arrogance*

and folly. All these evils come from inside and make a man "unclean" (NIV).

When we allow our minds to meditate on unwholesome or impure thoughts, they will eventually be reproduced in our attitudes, words, and actions. It is our choice to protect our minds from evil and to develop righteous character. *Who we are* is formed in the secret corridors of our minds by the thoughts that we choose—by the meditations we consistently permit.

We all have the same basic life experiences. Our circumstances may certainly be less than ideal. They can involve discomfort, disappointment, distress—even disaster. Difficulties and people irritate or please us. However, we can change our mind-set and face every problem as a challenge. We can choose positive and productive attitudes. As we discipline our thoughts, our perspective can be changed, our emotions can be controlled, and our character created. We can turn our obstacles into opportunities, our stumbling blocks into stepping stones, our responses into positive action.

Questions for Practical Application

1. Can you identify individuals who have influenced you by their excellence of disposition while enduring difficult circumstances?

2. From your observations, what is the difference between a bad attitude and a good attitude?

3. What practical steps do you intend to take to improve your outlook in your present situation?

4. Are your attitudes based on self-serving motives? Does self-centeredness or self-pity dictate your mindset?

5. In what ways do you intend to bring control to your thoughts and emotions?

6. Are you disappointed with the character you have created by your choices? How will you proceed to make desired changes?

Challenge

Finally, brothers, whatever is true, whatever is noble, whatever is right, whatever is pure, whatever is lovely, whatever is admirable—if anything is excellent or praiseworthy—think about such things.

Philippians 4:8, NIV

Chapter Five

Determining the Consequences

*The strongest principle of growth
lies in the human choice.*
George Elliot

*More than anything else, I believe
it's our decisions, not the conditions of our lives,
that determine our destiny.*
Anthony Robbins

When Moses spoke of life and death, blessing and cursing, in Deuteronomy 30:19, the reference is not only to the end result. Our choices determine if the pathway of our life will produce virtue, vitality, and victory—or breed darkness, despair, and death. We need to consider the journey, the road we travel, and the life we live day by day. Some choose the way that produces life; others choose the way of the living dead. Every choice we make creates either positive or negative results.

In the following oppositional questions, we can clearly see the consequences of our choices. Honest answers will also reveal whether we are walking in the way of life or the way of death.

Is it the way of life to be a victorious or a defeated Christian?

We become victorious believers because we make a conscious choice to be so. For example, even though the Bible is a living book it will not jump into our hands demanding, "Read me!" We must make the decision to pick it up, read it, and apply it. The life of victory means that believers will make choices that produce godly character and fruitfulness.

The life of victory means that believers will make choices that produce godly character and fruitfulness.

If we are defeated in our Christian walk, it is because we have chosen to be. Lack of spiritual disciplines, uncontrolled negative imaginations, and fouling habits produce guilt, discourage-

78

ment, disillusionment, and eventually barrenness of soul.

A bumper sticker reads, "Sometimes we're the bug...and sometimes we're the windshield!" There are moments when we feel strong and confident, well able to face every obstacle. Then there are those other occasions when we feel that we have been squashed—every hope dashed. We are left mangled by the crashes and crushes of our circumstances or personal failures.

We may be tempted to pack it in when things don't go our way. We would like to throw up our hands in despair and complain, "The problem is too difficult!" We may draw back and wring our hands in dismay. There are people who may feel victimized and perhaps with good reason. Some may use those experiences as excuses to continue in failure, rather than choose solutions for success.

It is not the one who falls who is the failure, but rather the one who fails to get up again and keep going. Judas and Peter both denied Christ. They both were filled with deep remorse and anguish for their dark deeds. But only Peter truly repented and went to face his risen Master. The courage to repent, pick up the pieces, lift up our heads, and overcome is our choice.

In 2 Corinthians 4:8, 9 Paul described some of the pressures that he was experiencing. He said,

> *We are pressed on every side by troubles, but not crushed and broken. We are perplexed because we don't know why things happen as they do, but we don't give up and quit. We are hunted down, but God never abandons us. We get knocked down, but we get up again and keep going* (TLB).

This passage exemplifies the response of Paul even in critical situations. In spite of difficulties, he was victorious in Christ. He made this confession in Romans 8:37, "...*in all these things we are more than conquerors through him that loved us.*" Founding our faith upon God's promises, we can choose to lift up our hearts, turn negatives to positives, death to life.

Is it the way of life to live with peace of mind or to be burdened with anxiety?

Those who endure the slow death of suffocating anxiety do so because of their choices. It has been noted that ninety-eight percent of the things we worry about will never happen, and the two percent that will happen, will never arrive the way we envisioned!

In the Sermon on the Mount recorded in Matthew 6:25, 26 Jesus taught,

> ...Take no thought for your life, what ye shall eat, or what ye shall drink; nor yet for your body, what ye shall put on. Is not the life more than meat, and the body than raiment? Behold the fowls of the air: for they sow not, neither do they reap, nor gather into barns; yet your heavenly Father feedeth them. Are ye not much better than they?

On one occasion I was speaking with a woman who was overcome with anxiety about innumerable petty details. As she shared her fears, we prayed for each one. She was greatly relieved. The following day, however, when I spoke with her I dared to ask how she was doing. She started the same tune again. In astonishment, I reminded her that we had carefully laid all those burdens before the Lord. What more could she worry about? To my amazement, she replied, "I guess I'm worried because I have nothing to worry about."

A friend with whom I traveled on a mission trip in Asia had a succinct way of summing up my anxious moments. She would say, "Now just think about the worst thing that could happen to us." Well, of course, I thought that we might die! But then again for the child of God, what could be so terrible about that? She had caught me.

In Philippians 4:6, 7 we have a command and a promise:

> *Do not be anxious about anything, but in everything, by prayer and petition, with thanksgiving, present your requests to God. And the peace of God, which*

transcends all understanding, will guard your hearts and your minds in Christ Jesus (NIV).

The secular definition of peace is the "absence of conflict." The peace that we have in Christ is far more comprehensive. This powerful force is released by our relationship with, and trust in the Person—the Prince of Peace. For the child of God, peace is much more like a river. Although the surface can be swept with turbulence, underneath the current is ever flowing and unaffected by the waves above.

For the child of God, peace is much more like a river.

In Colossians 3:15 we are exhorted to *"...let the peace of God rule in your hearts... and be ye thankful."* Living in the peace of God enhances our health, happiness, and holiness. The journey walked in peace is on the road of life.

Is it the way of life to overcome or to yield to temptation?

We are never tempted to do those things we don't like. I have never yet been tormented with desire to wash dishes! The truth is that we don't really fall into temptation; we dive into it! Sometimes we don't disclose our secret failings because, in a morbid sort of way, we enjoy them. This reality applies to every vice from anger to lust, from bitterness to self-pity, and every other depravity.

When we first yield to temptation we search for justification. Our reasoning soon provides the excuses but cannot soothe the pain of a tortured conscience. Although the temporary thrill of titillating sensualities may seduce, they eventually leave us wounded, riddled with guilt, and desperately alone.

The Bible gives a clear description of the process of temptation in James 1:13-15:

When tempted, no one should say, 'God is tempting me.' For God cannot be

tempted by evil, nor does he tempt any-
one; but each one is tempted when, by his
own evil desire, he is dragged away and
enticed. Then, after desire has conceived,
it gives birth to sin; and sin, when it is
full-grown, gives birth to death (NIV).

When Jesus was tempted, He rebuked Satan by using the Word of God (Matthew 4:3-10). Although He was tempted in all points as we are, yet He overcame. Now He can empower us also to overcome Satan and his seductions.

For we have not an high priest which
cannot be touched with the feeling of our
infirmities; but was in all points tempted
like as we are, yet without sin. Let us
therefore come boldly unto the throne of
grace, that we may obtain mercy, and
find grace to help in time of need
(Hebrews 4:15, 16).

Temptation always appeals to our five senses and arrives in the present crisis. On one occa-

Temptation always appeals to our five senses and arrives in the present crisis.

sion, together with friends, I had done some sightseeing and was now heading home for supper. It had been a long time since lunch and my stomach was complaining. That's when a friend showed up with a box of donuts. Covered with sugar, full of fat and grease but with a tantalizing aroma, they were set down in front of me. Every one of those donuts shouted, "Eat me!" What was I to do? Of course I had one.

The first bite, however, told me I had made a mistake. It was cold, stale, dry, and tasted like sawdust! Out of politeness I had to finish it, but in so doing ruined my appetite for the delicious and healthy supper that was waiting for me.

It was the story of Eden all over again. The tempter tantalizes with stuff that looks so good and screams, "Try me!" But after we have tasted, our mouths are filled with sand, and our hearts with guilt. How thankful I am for the cleansing power of Christ that convicts us of our sin; and when we repent, He brings forgiveness and healing to our hearts. 1 John 1:9 provides this promise: *"If we confess our sins, he is faithful and just to forgive us our sins, and to cleanse us from all unrighteousness."*

When we choose to overcome temptation, we are opting for the higher road. It may not be as glamorous, but it certainly produces the lasting joy for which we truly long. It is on the path of a clear conscience where life overflows.

Is it the way of life to be lazy or to be productive?

There is something placed within the human heart that longs to create, to achieve, to accomplish. An ancient adage states, "The way to kill a man is to give him money without work." Freeloading without responsibility eventually damages the necessary sense of personal human value. Why then do we often choose the path of laziness, forfeiting our own dignity?

In 2 Thessalonians 3:10-12, Paul admonished the believers to fill their lives with productive activities:

For even when we were with you, we gave you this rule: 'If a man will not work, he shall not eat.' We hear that some among you are idle. They are not busy; they are busybodies. Such people we command and urge in the Lord Jesus Christ to settle down and earn the bread they eat (NIV).

John Wesley, the founder of the Methodist movement, was greatly used by God to preach the gospel throughout the British Isles in the eighteenth century. Early in his ministry he determined that he would accomplish something of value with every minute of his life. Considering that he had no access to modern media or transportation, his achievements were phenomenal. In the last fifty-two years of his life it is estimated that he journeyed over 250,000 miles mostly on horseback, and preached some 42,000 sermons.

Being an avid reader he applied himself to study, even authoring several books as he rode his horse! Besides preaching twice each day (and often three or four times), he organized and directed the fledgling Methodist movement. He championed worthy moral causes, powerfully affecting even the highest echelons of British politics. Probably no other person accomplished more and exerted greater influence for good in that period of history. He made minutes count.

Time and life are incredibly valuable commodities.

Time and life are incredibly valuable commodities. They can never be replaced. It is amazing that people will waste huge blocks of their life watching worthless, corrupt movies and inane blather. In the name of entertainment and relaxation, they permit the beauty of real-life caring and real-life sharing to be stolen from them. While living in a world of make-believe and pretense, they open their minds to be manipulated by unprofitable and unscrupulous programming.

Some people spend their existence surfing the internet; others squander their time in unproductive activities that are beneficial to no one. I overheard a friend say that killing time is not murder; it is suicide. A lyricist penned, "The bore chatters on, never losing his breath; his way to kill time is to talk it to death!"[8]

We must, of course, seek balance between work and play. We need time for rest and recreation. It is important to take time to love people, family, and friends. Reaching out to others is not spending time; it is investing it. There is a vast difference between healthy relaxation and the emptiness of a wasted life.

The reward is far superior both to ourselves and to the world around us when we seek to be fruitful. Even for those who must endure great physical limitations, whose achievements may be the performance of simple survival tasks, the spirit grows stronger after each accomplishment. Purpose fills life with meaning.

Is it the way of life to be thankful or to be ungrateful?

There are some individuals who exist with little appreciation for the blessings surrounding them. Some people never see the beautiful moments of life because they are blinded by their ungratefulness. By contrast, the darkest night can be like brilliant day in the hearts of those who have learned to be grateful for the seemingly insignificant treasures along the path of life. An Estonian proverb suggests, "He who does not thank for little, will not thank for much."

Often parents are amazed by the lack of gratitude expressed by their children. They look at designer jeans lying in a heap on bedroom floors and watch the mountains of food disappear off plates, vainly awaiting a word of thanks. Then we hear these same parents complain about the government, the boss, the co-worker, and the neighbor. A dad says that the car is too old or too small; a mom says that in three walk-in closets she doesn't have a thing to wear. They both exclaim, "I wonder where the kids learned such ungratefulness!"

Throughout the Bible we have many references to those who gave thanks, including our Lord Himself. In command and example we are admonished, *"In every thing give thanks: for this is the will of God in Christ Jesus concerning you"* (1 Thessalonians 5:18). Again we read, *"Giving thanks always for all things unto God and the Father in the name of our Lord Jesus Christ"* (Ephesians 5:20).

When we look up and out beyond our greed, there is no end of blessings for which to be thankful.

When we look up and out beyond our greed, there is no end of blessings for which to be thankful. When we know Jesus Christ as our Savior, when we have His assurance of eternal life, we have the ultimate possession, which far outweighs anything money could ever buy. It is then that our hearts are free to start counting all the temporal acquisitions of lesser importance.

Some time ago I received an e-mail that out-lined the oft-overlooked abundance I have in comparison to millions of others who share this planet. It is a reminder of the awesome privileges that must never be taken for granted.

- If you have food in the refrigerator, clothes on your back, a roof overhead and a place to sleep, you are richer than 75 percent of this world.
- If you have money in the bank, in your wallet, and spare change in a dish some-place, you are among the top 8 percent of the world's wealthy.
- If you woke up this morning with more health than illness, you are more blessed than the million who will not survive this week.
- If you have never experienced the danger of battle, the agony of torture, or the pangs of starvation, you are ahead of 500 million people in the world.
- If you can attend a church meeting without fear of harassment, arrest, torture, or

death, you are more blessed than three billion people in the world.

There is a story about a pastor with the reputation of always being thankful. One stormy Sunday morning his wife was ill. He drove alone along the muddy road on his way to the service, only to be stopped by a flat tire. By the time it was changed he was covered in mud. Arriving late at the church he realized he had forgotten his key. After crawling through a window and ripping the trousers of his muddy suit, he opened the door to let in the only two elderly parishioners who had braved the storm to attend. Both had forgotten their offering. As they sat waiting one whispered to the other, "I wonder what he will be thankful for today." Their courageous pastor stepped to the pulpit and declared, "I am so thankful—that every day is not like today!"

I know of no more effective way to be uplifted on a discouraging and difficult day than to express gratefulness and appreciation. Praise and thanksgiving to God open the springs of living water.

Is it the way of life to be happy or to be unhappy?

People who are on a search for happiness often overlook the fundamental fact that happiness begins with a decision. People go through nearly identical circumstances. Some complain their entire journey; others bounce through with a smile. It is the power of choice that makes the difference.

There are a few folk to whom one would never dare to ask, "How are you?" We know the answer before hearing the barrage of grousing and bitterness. Conversing with some people creates the sinking sensation of being sucked into a cesspool of negativism. After a few minutes of listening to the complaints, it is a relief to flee! Others, however, are a joy to be near. Their conversations vibrate with good cheer; just seeing their countenance brings a flood of relief and encouragement. Their positive words bring life to all they meet. People are drawn to them because their obvious joy of living is contagious.

An elderly woman told me a long time ago, "Make sure you marry a man who has learned to be happy while he is still single. If he isn't happy before you marry him, he surely won't be happy afterwards." Marriage, promotions, or possessions may enhance happiness but never create it.

Marriage, promotions, or possessions may enhance happiness but never create it.

King David experienced the heavy pressures of guiding his kingdom through a perilous period of history. At times unscrupulous backstabbers and treacherous enemies surrounded him; other times he found himself very alone and fragile. He knew the whole range of human emotions just as we do, yet in Psalm 42:4 David sang, *"Why then be downcast? Why be discouraged and sad? Hope in God! I shall yet praise him again. Yes, I shall again praise him for his help"* (TLB). He determined to lift up his heart and be glad in spite of it all.

The happiest people are also the most gracious and generous. It is a principle that as we pour our love out to others, happiness and blessings pour back on us. A stingy soul is often embittered and cold. Selfishness always breeds discontent. By contrast, generosity brings blessing and joy. The Bible says in Proverbs 11:25, "*A generous man will prosper; he who refreshes others will himself be refreshed*" (NIV). We can choose to reach out of ourselves to show an abundance of mercy and goodwill to everyone who crosses our path.

Definitions of happiness abound. However, happiness will find the one who makes the choice to leave sorrows behind, live the moment, and lift the heart in praise.

Is it the way of life to forgive or to carry offense?

Unforgiveness is powerfully destructive, both psychologically and physiologically. Those who are easily and continually offended multiply their own wounds. If they internalize the anger and offences, the resulting bitterness devours the mind like a cancer in the soul.

It is a true proverb that we become the slave of those we hate. When we carry grudges, our thoughts are often consumed with images and imaginations of those we have permitted to offend us. In the chambers of our minds we hold conferences where we rehearse all we would like to say or do to them if we only had the chance. Meanwhile, the objects of our obsessive grudges are having a great day. They may even be blissfully oblivious to our annoyance. We hurt no one but ourselves.

"Forgiveness is like releasing a prisoner and discovering the prisoner was you."

Basically forgiveness is a choice—a choice to let the offences go. An ancient proverb states, "Forgiveness is like releasing a prisoner and discovering the prisoner was you." When Jesus was discussing forgiveness He made some startling and serious statements. In Matthew 6:14, 15 He said, *"For if ye forgive men their trespasses, your heavenly Father will also forgive you: But if ye forgive not men their trespasses, neither will your Father forgive your trespasses."*

Within the space of six months, shortly after my mother turned 62 years of age, her life was dramatically and radically changed by tragedy and loss. Her second son, my brother, upon whom the care of the family farm, his wife and children, and my parents' welfare was dependent, was killed by two escaped convicts. She, as a key witness, had to testify at the trial of his murderers. My father, who had a type of Alzheimer's disease, was put into a nursing home. The family farm, which my father's own hands had tamed from the wild prairie, was sold.

Through it all her faith in God remained firm. She chose both forgiveness and compassion to those who had brought her so much pain. With dignity and poise her courage and good cheer brought inspiration and strength to others. In spite of everything, her heart was free.

While counseling with those who are experiencing depression, I ask them if they are carrying bitterness or unforgiveness. The answer invariably is affirmative. Most people can actually tell when the depression started and pinpoint the situation when they permitted bitterness to tak root. They had made the choice to carry the grudge that was now destroying them.

In Matthew 5:44, Jesus not only told His disciples to forgive, but to bless those who had offended them: *"...Love your enemies, bless them that curse you, do good to them that hate you, and pray for them which despitefully use you, and persecute you."* When we choose to forgive and earnestly pray for God to bless those who have injured us, the choking chain of bitterness is destroyed.

It is important to note the difference between forgiveness and trust. The entire process of forgiveness is released to work in us when we make the choice to forgive. Granting pardon has to do with past wrongs, perceived or literal. By contrast, trust has to do with the future and must be built by positive relational experience.

Some people are afraid to forgive because they feel if they truly forgive they must also trust those who have wronged them. That is not true. :d. Interestingly, when we compare werful forces of love, forgiveness, : find that trust is by far the most fragile. Broken trust is the most difficult to mend—but possible with God's help.

Anger and offence are often our reaction to hurts and rejection. Both bear the sour fruit of bitterness. Someone once remarked, "Every minute we are angry, we lose sixty seconds of happiness." When we repent and forgive, the fangs are pulled from our anger. The chains of offence are broken. It is then we are freed to truly live.

In all of life's situations, we are presented with options. One way or another we will—we do—make choices. However, there will be consequences to every decision we make. The attitudes and actions we choose will determine the fruit that will be produced. What shall the harvest be? That depends on us.

Questions for Practical Application

1. Are you a victorious or defeated Christian?

2. Are you filled with peace or burdened with care?

3. Are you overcoming temptation or yielding to temptation?

4. Are you a lazy or productive individual?

5. Are you a thankful or ungrateful person?

6. Are you happy or unhappy?

7. Do you live with forgiveness or offense?

8. What choices are you going to make to create life-fulfilling consequences?

Challenge

For if ye forgive men their passes, your heavenly Father will also forgive you: But if ye forgive not men their trespasses, neither will your Father forgive your trespasses.

Matthew 6:14, 15

Chapter Six

Loving to Live Life

*Let him who would enjoy a good future
waste none of his present.*

Roger Babson

When it came time to die, I had not lived.

Tombstone epitaph

Many people go through life without really living. They exist. They eat and sleep. They function. But there is no depth of purpose or *joie de vivre*. Almost like manikins on a roller coaster, they sway and rock but enjoy nothing.

There are those who look back on a life lived without purpose, without significance. What living they have done has only been through the antics of the other actors dancing on the screen. For some folks, the would-be dreams, the hoped-for plans lie tangled in the debris of indecision.

We can make a difference, not only in our own lives, but also in our world by the choices we make. We can live with fulfillment and impact. Day-by-day existence can move from surviving to thriving. Destiny can be experienced while the journey is still in progress.

Investing for maximum value

Time—we measure it in minutes, miles, milliseconds. Every heartbeat, every breath personalizes the limits, the brevity of our allotted living. No matter how long we live, life is short.

Every day is precious. The hours that pass are forever gone. We will never have another chance to walk this road. The past is as money spent; the future is but a promissory note.

We have these moments to turn into profit or loss....

The present is as ready cash to be invested. We have these moments to turn into profit or loss—the profit of a life well spent or the loss of opportunities that are forever gone.

It has been noted that no one on their deathbed wishes that they might have spent more time at the office. Rather, many are the regrets for lost moments of caring, of sharing, of touching family and friends. Go ahead, tell a precious one that you love them, brush a tear from a lonely heart, hold a child by the hand, listen to the aged. Take a few moments to inhale the fragrance of the flowers, to examine their exquisite design. Watch with wonder as the sun splashes radiant hues across the sky while bidding the day farewell. It is our choice to make worthwhile investments of our time.

The way we choose to spend our money indicates cherished values of our hearts. We have exchanged huge chunks of our existence to possess money and the materials it can buy. We have spent brains and brawn for the commodities that we purchase. What then will create life-producing returns from material possessions?

Theodore L. Cayler stated, "I never knew a child of God bankrupted by his benevolence.

What we keep we may lose, but what we give to Christ, we are sure to keep." We know we can't take it with us, but we can send it ahead—by our generosity to those in need. Jesus said we could, in Matthew 6:20, "...*lay up for yourselves treasures in heaven, where neither moth nor rust doth corrupt, and where thieves do not break through nor steal.*" We can make the decision to funnel our financial resources into eternal causes.

Some of the most gifted people I have met have never tried to develop their talents to their full potential. I have been amazed at some of the excuses that are used to keep magnificent abilities buried. Some only play their musical instruments for their own enjoyment to avoid criticism or comparison; others feel too timid to sing in front of someone else. One woman burned beautiful paintings because she was afraid her family would not want them. Others don't want to make the effort or pay the price to develop skills.

We can choose to use or lose the capacities we have been given. We can make the decision to reach out of our comfort zones and invest our strengths and abilities to bring encouragement and blessing to others.

By contrast, there are individuals who struggle with great personal weaknesses including physical, emotional, or intellec-

We can choose to use or lose the capacities we have been given.

tual limitations. Rather than excuse, hide, or resent their incapacities, they have permitted their vulnerability to bring hope and help to many. By choosing to extend beyond themselves, their struggles have challenged others to excellence.

In Luke 9:24, 25, Jesus was instructing His followers about eternal principles:

> *"If you try to hang on to your life, you will lose it. But if you give up your life for my sake, you will save it. And what do you benefit if you gain the whole world but are yourself lost or destroyed?"* (TLB).

When we determine to invest our time, finances, and talents making God's principles our priorities, richness and fulfillment will be produced. Everything that has been placed within our hands can be used to benefit those around us. Our lives find lasting value by bringing life to others.

A life well lived

One man told of his dream to one day— some day—climb a mountain. After years of wishing, an unexpected opportunity was suddenly available. He was scared to death. He worried. He hesitated. He fussed. Finally he dared. The exhilaration of struggling to the summit jarred him to the reality that he was living his dream. He began to live and love the moment. The platitudes of boredom and purposelessness fell from him. From the mountain peak he determined to continue to reach out of humdrum existence into the challenge of living with enthusiasm.

Author Jack London is credited with the following quote:

I would rather be ashes than dust!

I would rather that my spark died out in a brilliant blaze than it should be stifled by dry rot.

I would rather be a superb meteor, every atom of me in magnificent glow, than a sleepy and permanent planet.

The proper function of man is to live, not to exist.

I shall not waste my days trying to prolong them.

I shall use my time.[9]

A number of years ago an older man was preparing to work on a building project with missionary friends in Uganda. Although I do not know his identity, he gave the following address at his local church before leaving America. The missionary, Mrs. May Dodzweit, included it in a monthly newsletter.

I am over the hill. I am sixty-six years old. I have a total hip replacement so my right hip is stainless steel. My left knee is fifty percent gone with osteoarthritis and will have to be replaced. Thank the Lord for replacement parts! Both of my shoulders are bad and I cannot put my arms up or backwards. I have sugar diabetes and I take a total of up to two hundred units of insulin by three injections per day. I test my blood by pinpricking my finger. I have bad feet that hurt when I walk too much. But I have an enormous project to do in Uganda. I'm not sure that I can get it done before I reach seventy years old, God's allotted time for us, so I may have to borrow a couple more years from God out of my Eternal Rest. But don't feel sorry for me, because I have the privilege to do this enormous job for the Lord. What is your excuse?

When I started to read the letter I thought this man had one foot in the grave and the other on a banana peel! As I read on my admiration grew, for he had learned the secret of living life. Every person has talents, virtues, or personality with which to touch others. When we choose to live a self-centered life, we rob the world of the love and joy our gifts could generate.

There are people who have wasted years complaining, being angry, unhappy, and offended. They have chosen to let time slip by while they have wallowed in self-pity and despair. Blaming their lack of fulfillment on circumstances or other people, they refuse to accept responsibility and

The future can be changed. We can start now.

acknowledge that they are the tragic result of their own choices. They have invested their life in digging their own graves!

The future can be changed. We can start now. Whatever tragedies of loss and waste might be in our yesterdays, our choices today can change our tomorrows. We must not let the regrets for past failures overwhelm our decisions to rise higher now. Someone gave me this little poem. I do not

know who the author is but it well summarizes
my sentiments:

Humpty Dumpty sat on the wall,
Humpty Dumpty had a great fall.
All the king's horses and all the king's
men,
Couldn't put Humpty together again.
Now to understand the moral of this
rhyme we undertake,
We must not strive if we're made of stuff
that breaks.
For thin skins and tender feelings and
shells made of soft stuff,
Will break into pieces when the going
gets rough.
For the tumble will come when new
heights we achieve,
Then all the king's men and their horses
can't the breakage relieve.
So pick up that egg and dust off the dirt,
You're not dead, just hurt.
Get back on that wall, don't lie there and
beg,

Take another step higher and prove
·you're a good egg![10]

When we surrender our being to Jesus Christ
as our Savior, we begin to discover true purpose
and value for our lives—He is the Way of Life.
The pursuit of God is the highest purpose of
humanity. Philippians 4:13 affirms, "*I can do all
things through Christ which strengtheneth me.*"
By following His word, His teaching and example, we not only walk the way of life, but we
have the assurance of our destiny—eternal life.

In this poem entitled *With Christ*, we are
reminded that we do not walk alone as we press
on toward the reward of a life well lived.

> It's not so much where you have
> been, but where you are going.
>
> It's not so much that you have
> hurt, but that you will heal.
>
> It's not so much what you have
> done, but what you will do.
>
> It's not so much whether you

have fallen, but whether you will get up.

It's not so much who you are, but who you will be.

He cares for you.

He says, "Follow me."[11]

Questions for Practical Application

1. Can you name individuals who have impacted you by their zest for living?

2. What are some areas where you have chosen mediocrity instead of enthusiasm for life? What changes do you hope to implement?

3. What do you consider to be the greatest achievements of your life? Will your present choices continue to produce quality of life and character?

4. What are the greatest regrets or disappointments of your life? Will your present decisions result in reproducing regrets?

5. What would you like written on your epitaph? What choices will you make now to attain that goal?

Challenge

If you try to hang on to your life, you will lose it. But if you give up your life for my sake, you will save it. And what do you benefit if you gain the whole world but are yourself lost or destroyed?

Luke 9:24, 25; TLB

Conclusion

It was going to be a bad day. I knew it from the moment that I came to consciousness. I was tired before I opened my eyes. The dripping rain didn't help my mood. Then I looked in the mirror. Not just a bad day—a bad hair day!

The morning news was depressing. The toaster jammed. The toast burned. The phone rang with more depressing news. Now the burnt toast was cold.

That's when I saw him through my kitchen window. With great effort my neighbor descended the steps of his home, clinging to the handrail for support. Although he is a relatively young man, the doctors can do little for his damaged back. He slowly crawled into his truck, his face etched in pain. Almost every day he drives a hundred kilometers for therapy. Even after a year of treatment there has been virtually no improvement in his physical condition.

Compassion for my neighbor caused me to reflect on the bountiful blessings God had given to me. Suddenly it was a good day. Cold, burnt toast isn't all that bad. I had food to eat. I bounced down the steps to the utility room to throw in a load of laundry. I would choose to make this day an extraordinary day—the best day of the rest of my life.

* * *

God has granted us the tremendous power to choose *who* we will be. Our character and our core values are results of our choices. In face of every human problem we can determine our attitude and our response. We cannot escape from this ultimate personal responsibility.

When we make decisions and positive actions according to His Word, the hand of God is released to work in our circumstances. He has put within our reach the option to seize the opportunities for salvation, for liberation, for change, and for direction.

Rather than viewing the world as musts and must-nots, we can walk in the way that brings truth and beauty. We can be greatly motivated to righteousness when seeking those activities that produce life instead of death. By living with the end in view, we can maximize the joy of the journey.

When we choose excellence of attitude, we facilitate the capacity to respond to every situation with purpose and poise. Even when life seems unfair and circumstances are disagreeable, positive attitudes and wholesome thoughts bring inner contentment and maximum benefit.

Every choice we make has a consequence. The results will produce either character and virtue or emptiness and despair. We can be victorious, overcoming believers living in "*...the peace of God that passeth all understanding...*" (Philippians 4:7). Gratitude, forgiveness, and happiness are choices of the heart.

Life is a precious gift from God. What we do

with our life can be our gift back to Him. Don't waste another precious minute of time on this earth. Make the choice; take the challenge; create the change—love living life.

The Gift of Salvation

If you have never given your life to Christ, I sincerely urge you to surrender to Him today. According Romans 3:23, "*...all have sinned, and come short of the glory of God.*"

The Bible tells us that peace with God is received by turning to Him from our sins. In Romans 10:9, 10, 13 we read:

> "*...if you confess with your mouth, 'Jesus is Lord,' and believe in your heart that God raised him from the dead, you will be saved. For it is with your heart that you believe and are justified, and it is with your mouth that you confess and are saved. ... For whosoever shall call upon the name of the Lord shall be saved.*" (NIV).

You can receive His life now by repentance and faith. Pray this simple prayer:

"Lord, I know I have sinned. I believe You are the Son of God and that You died on the cross to forgive my sins. I believe You have risen from the dead with power to give me a transformed life. Please forgive me, change my heart, and set me free. I surrender the control of my will to You. Help me to follow You. In Jesus' Name. Amen."

Read the Bible and pray every day. Find others who love Jesus who can help you to follow Him. With your hand in the hand of Jesus, you will finish your journey with joy.

Notes

1 Newspaper, source unknown

2 Steven Covey, *The 7 Habits of Highly Effective People,* (New York, NY: Simon and Schuster, 1989), 71.

3 Ibid., 73.

4 Viktor E. Frankl, *Man's Search for Meaning: An Introduction to Logotheraphy,* Preface by Gordon W. Allport, (Boston, MA: Beacon Press, 1992), 75.

5 Charles Swindoll, *Strengthening Your Grip,* (Waco, TX: Bantam book / published by arrangement with Word, Inc., 1986), 177.

6 Author unknown

7 Elizabeth George, *Loving God with All Your Mind,* (Eugene, OR: Harvest House Publishers, 1994/2005), 42.

8 Author unknown

9 Jack London (1876-1916) "Jack London's Credo", Commentary by Clarice Stasz, document maintained at: http://london. sonoma.edu/credo.html: last update January 19, 1999

10 Author unknown

11 Author unknown

Please visit Anita's Web site,

www.inspirationministries.net

for a complete catalogue of her
music CDs, DVDs, and other
ministry information.

Also available from Inspiration Ministries:

Other Books:

Above the Storm

Music CDs:

Grace

Thread of Hope

Mercy

He Loved Me Enough

Sermons:

Storms (DVD)

Connected (CD Three-Pack Series)

Anita's Personal Testimony (DVD)

Visit

www.inspirationministries.net

to order today!